HR Hazards
Model answers to 70 HR problems

By Daniel Barnett

The Employment Law Library

All books in the Employment Law Library are sent for free to members of the HR Inner Circle.

1. Employee Investigations

2. GDPR for HR Professionals

3. Preventing and Defending Employee Stress Claims

4. Employment Tribunal Time Limits

5. Deconstructing TUPE

6. Changing Terms & Conditions

7. Constructive Dismissal

8. Resolving Grievances

9. HR Hazards

Published by Employment Law Services Limited, Unit 3, Chequers Farm, Chequers Lane, Watford, Hertfordshire WD25 0LG

ISBN: 978-1-913925-02-4

EMPLOYMENT
LAW
MATTERS

Subscribe to
Daniel Barnett's podcast
EMPLOYMENT LAW MATTERS
via iTunes, Spotify, or your
favourite podcast player

WWW.DANIELBARNETT.CO.UK/PODCAST

DANIEL BARNETT
BARRISTER

THE UK'S LEADING YOUTUBE CHANNEL FOR LAW EXPLAINER VIDEOS

BIT.LY/**YOUTUBELEGAL**

About the Author

Daniel Barnett is a leading employment law barrister practising from Outer Temple Chambers. With 25 years' experience defending public and private sector employers against employment claims, he has represented a Royal Family, several international airlines, FTSE-100 companies and various NHS Trusts and local authorities. Employee clients include David & Victoria Beckham's nanny and Paul Mason (subject of the ITV documentary 'Britain's Fattest Man').

Daniel is a past chair of the Employment Lawyers' Association's publishing committee and electronic services working party. He is the author or co-author of eight books, including the Law Society Handbook on Employment Law (currently in its 8th edition). He is the creator of the Employment Law (UK) mailing list, an email alerter bulletin service sending details of breaking news in employment law three times a week to 30,000 recipients.

Legal directories describe him as 'extremely knowledgeable and [he] can absorb pages of instructions at lightning speed', 'involved in a number of highly contentious matters', 'singled out for his work for large blue-chip companies', 'combination of in-depth legal knowledge, pragmatism, quick response times and approachability', 'inexhaustible', 'tenacious', 'knowledgeable', and 'an excellent advocate'.

He is one of the leading speakers and trainers on the employment law and HR circuit. He has presented seminars for the House of Commons, the BBC, Oxford University, HSBC, Barclays Bank, Ocado, and dozens of other organisations in-house. In 2013, 2014, 2016, and 2019 he designed — and was the sole speaker at — the Employment Law MasterClass national tour.

As well as full-time practice as a barrister and speaker, Daniel is the founder of the HR Inner Circle – a membership club for smart, ambitious HR Professionals. In 2007, he co-founded CPD Webinars Ltd, then the UK's leading webinar training company for lawyers, and sold it to Thomson Reuters in 2011.

Daniel is widely sought after as a commentator in both broadcast and print media on all legal issues. Since 2010 he has presented the Legal Hour on LBC Radio. In 2019, he launched Employment

Law Matters, a weekly podcast with short explanations of employment law topics. Subscribe at www.danielbarnett.co.uk/podcast

www.danielbarnett.co.uk
Outer Temple Chambers
Strand, London

Acknowledgments

This is the ninth in my series of small employment law books. They are designed to give HR professionals and those without a formal law degree a solid grounding in a subject that they won't learn about through normal avenues.

I'd like to thank Jennie Hargrove for her help with the content, Tincuta Moscaliuc for the layout and design, Aaron Gaff for proofreading and Maria Rodriguez for converting the book to the formats needed for Amazon.

I would also like to thank Emma Vernon, Penelope Douglass, Patrick McNamee,Fran Trousdale, Olivia Flattery, Jean Hall, and Paul Helsby, all of whom commented on an early draft of this book and helped by brining their many years' experience as HR professionals to bear. All are members of www.hrinnercircle.co.uk and I learn as much from them as I hope they learn from me.

Daniel Barnett
April 2021

Table of Contents

WORKING TIME AND MINIMUM WAGE

What's the law for taking time off for doctor, dentist and other appointments?

Many employers have no difficulty with diligent employees coming in half an hour later, by arrangement, once or twice a year. Some employers would encourage the individual to make an appointment outside working hours or, if that is not possible, to take annual leave or unpaid leave. Ideally, employees could be encouraged to take such appointments at the start or end of the day to limit disruption.

However, there is no legal right for the employee to take time off for doctor, dentist or other appointments unless:

1. it's an antenatal appointment for a woman who is pregnant; or,

2. the individual qualifies as disabled and giving them time off work would be a reasonable adjustment.

But apart from those two exceptions there is no right to take time off work during working hours for doctor, dentist or other appointments. Therefore, if somebody does take time off without permission, they are taking unauthorised absence and you are entitled to discipline them.

If they've worked for you for more than two years and they've got the right to claim unfair dismissal dismissing them on the first occasion they took unauthorised absence would be unreasonable – it would be outside the range of reasonable responses. But you could legitimately give them a warning, and if they do it again after they've asked and you've said no, you can give them a final warning. If they then do it a third time, then dismissal will normally be a reasonable response.

We have an employee who is alleging that they are stressed from their workload, but they are not taking their breaks. They've consistently worked through lunch breaks. They've been told they need to make sure they take a break but they're just choosing not to. They're working long hours and they just generally say that they're struggling

with the workload. There's no difference between their workload and that of anybody else, it just seems to be that they aren't taking those breaks. They've been employed for eight months.

Is there any way that we can enforce that they take breaks to try to help the situation?

I don't think that making them take breaks, and thus making them feel even more overwhelmed by the work, is necessarily addressing the issue, although, of course, it is good practice to encourage people to take breaks.

I think a better approach is, bluntly, to recognise this employee possibly can't do the job. If other employees have the same workload and can manage it perfectly competently, and this one employee can't, it's a capability situation.

You could make a referral to occupational health if you think there may be a mental health issue involved. However, as long as you encourage them to take breaks, a court or tribunal will not criticise you for not forcing them to take breaks. As long as you've made breaks available, that's all that can reasonably be asked for and you're not going to have any difficulty defending that.

If we have hourly paid field engineers, can we pay them minimum wage rather than their hourly wage for travel time (at the beginning/end of the day and during the day)?

Payment for travel during the day is governed purely by the contract. If the contract provides for payment at a reduced rate, then that's the end of the issue.

Remember that with minimum wage, you're averaging out the total salary received every month. So you're not looking at any particular hour, and if during the other hours, the individuals earn a lot more than minimum wage, then reducing their pay for travel time, even down to zero, may not bring the average over the monthly period down to below minimum wage.

If they are peripatetic workers, and they are going to their first place of work and leaving their last place of work, then the definition of working time for the *Minimum Wage Regulations* (as opposed to the *Working Time Regulations*) does not cover the time they spend going to the first place of work, and back from the last place of work. So, an employer doesn't even need to worry about paying anything for that period of time.

A client I'm working with seems to not really engage with the Working Time Regulations. They're an events organisation and most of the employees have opted out of the 48-hour working week.

Due to the nature of the events, they sometimes have to work through their rest breaks. Other than ensuring that there is compensatory rest when possible, is there anything else that we need to bear in mind?

Regulation 12 of the *Working Time Regulations 1998* gives a right to a 20 minute break if someone has been working for six hours. Although there are reasons this can be missed and replaced with compensatory rest, set out in regulation 21, it's far from clear that events/hospitality employees fall within these exceptions.

That being the case, the obligation to offer compensatory rest doesn't arise, and instead the employees can simply bring a claim for breach of the *Working Time Regulations.* In practice, as long as they're paid additional salary so that they're essentially being paid extra for the lost rest break, there may be a technical breach of the Working Time Regulations, but the employees would be unable to prove any financial loss as a result, so they'd have a very limited claim.

A case in the Court of Appeal called *Santos Gomes v Higher Level Care [2018] IRLR 440* argued that you could get compensation for injured feelings arising out of the breach of rules relating to rest breaks. I was representing the employee and we lost so, as it stands, employees can't get compensation for upset and stress, etc.

GDPR

What's your view on routinely issuing a medical questionnaire as part of the starter pack in light of the General Data Protection Regulation (GDPR)?

There's nothing unlawful about having a medical questionnaire in a starter pack. You can't ask questions about medical conditions during the application stage (unless it's for the purpose of monitoring, or making reasonable adjustments to facilitate access to interviews etc), but you are entitled to ask them once a job offer is made, or once somebody has started in the role.

The problem is, what are you going to do if they refuse to fill it in? Although they won't have unfair dismissal rights when they first start, if you dismiss them for refusing, you're risking a disability discrimination claim. If you are a public sector employer, there are human rights issues to consider as well).

You should say on the questionnaire that they're going to fill in (and, presumably, sign) what you'll do with that data. For example, you may possibly share the data with Occupational Health if issues arise around fitness to work. So as long as you set out what you're going to be doing with the data (and that takes a bit of thought), then you're unlikely to run into any problems with the Information Commissioner.

One of our clients has had an employee leave and there's a dispute over final salary entitlement. We've tried to settle it through Acas but with no success. There's a possibility of litigation over this relatively small amount. The employee has now raised a subject access request (SAR) and they've asked for all dialogue between me and Acas on the client's behalf. Do I need to declare that, on the basis that my discussions with Acas are not admissible in court?

Good question, because it's not subject to legal advice privilege, which you don't have to disclose under a SAR. Under s18(6) of the *Employment Tribunals Act 1996*, it specifically says that nothing sent to Acas is admissible in a tribunal or a court without consent. But, of course, that doesn't mean that it's not admissible in the SAR. My instinct is that it is probably disclosable, unfortunately.

If you don't mind me adding: keep a sense of perspective. If it is, indeed, a 'relatively small amount', then perhaps you should just pay it rather than divert business time and money fighting over the 'relatively small amount'. Sometimes the fight just isn't worth the fight.

We've cancelled an employee's access to their company email after putting them on garden leave. They've now raised a SAR. Are they entitled to copies of all emails they sent through the company email system?

No, because you're only obliged under a SAR to provide information that you hold about somebody. The fact someone sent an email isn't information about them. It's not personal information. The fact that they're the sender or recipient of an email may be disclosable in a tribunal case, but it's not something you disclose in a SAR. The exception is if they are giving personal information about themselves by saying, for example, "I've had a bad day today because of X, Y, Z," or "I'm feeling a bit blue and moody because X, Y, Z." But if it's just a typical work email – for example, "Have you read the marketing report yet?" – that's not going to be covered by a SAR because it's not personal information.

Of course, the effort involved in reading through every one of their emails to see if it contains personal data is considerable. So perhaps give them access to their emails in a confidential data room, where they can't copy information, and let them read through everything and select what they want. This won't be a practical answer if you're worried they are thinking of joining a competitor, as you won't want *them* to have untrammelled access to client information, pricing information etc, but if that's not a concern, then this is a practical solution.

To what extent can an employer require a junior employee to alert them to potential data protection breaches by other members of staff?

In the same way that an employer can require an employee to do anything: as long as it's a reasonable and a lawful order (which it will be), it can go in the employee's contract and the employee can be required to do it.

I'm assuming the real question is: 'If they don't comply, can we dismiss them?' If there's nothing in the contract, it's quite difficult to compel somebody to do something. What you can do, by amending the disciplinary process, is say that you're introducing a new offence of failing to disclose a data protection breach, and say that going forward, it will be a disciplinary offence to fail to disclose a data protection breach by either yourself or a work colleague. I'd give a three- or six- month moratorium, where you say that in the first few months of implementing the new offence (so that everyone has time to get used to it), the maximum sanction you'll impose is a first written warning. Explain that after that, depending on the severity of the breach, you might regard it a lot more seriously.

In a SAR, are notes in a manager's notepad, prepared in advance of the meeting, disclosable? Does it fall within the scope of personal data?

The notes will fall within the scope of personal data because they will be about an employee and identifying the employee, and they would likely refer to the employee by name.

The real issue here is whether the manager's notepad amounts to a relevant filing system so as to be disclosable under a SAR. The answer to that is probably 'yes', if the individual can be identified relatively easily from the notepad. For example, if it's headed with their name, then it's obviously about them and therefore part of a relevant filing system. But also, bear in mind that whether or not it's a relevant filing system, these documents will be disclosable in tribunal proceedings anyway.

An employee has sent the entire company Dropbox to their personal email address, including client data. What action do we need to take?

Firstly, the company has an obligation under the GDPR to tell both the Information Commissioner and those people whose personal data has been compromised that this has happened.

Hopefully, in these circumstances, the employee has a proper employment contract that has restrictive covenants and confidential information clauses.

Call the individual to a disciplinary meeting for potential gross misconduct for the misuse of personal data. Investigate fully and if the allegations are proven (and there is no proper explanation), dismiss.

Previously, in our statement of terms, I've included a clause asking for consent to send somebody for a medical examination. Should that now come out of the contract? We've always had separate consent if we actually do want a medical report, but I'm just wondering whether that permission in the contract should be deleted now?

Information about health counts as 'sensitive' personal data, which means that you normally need express consent to be able to process it.

The problem, and this is where the Data Protection Act 2018 (which incorporates the GDPR) gets tricky, is that there are provisions within the GDPR that provide that where there is a significant disparity in bargaining power, the consent isn't valid. That's typically going to be the case in an employee-employer situation. So, despite the GDPR saying at one point that express consent is what you need, express consent in advance, which is not specific to the situation you're dealing with later on, probably isn't sufficient to comply with data protection laws if it's an employee/employer situation.

Having said that, there's no benefit in removing the consent clause from your contracts, as it's a useful fallback if you need something to argue. However, you may need to fall back on Article 9 of the GDPR. Article 9 provides that processing of personal data for the purpose of uniquely identifying data concerning health is prohibited. So that's the starting point: it's prohibited. It then goes on to say that this won't apply if the employee has given consent, but the problem is that consent is not consent where there's an inequality of bargaining power. Catch-22.

There is an exception. The prohibition on processing health data does <u>not</u> apply if it is necessary for the purposes of carrying out the obligations and exercising specific rights of the controller of the data subject – that's you – in the field of employment. So if it is necessary for carrying out employment related activities, it's probably going to be okay. The problem is that the Data Protection Act and the GDPR are just really badly drafted, and they make this whole area more complicated, and less certain, that they ought to be.

So, keep the consent clause in there, but recognise that the Information Commissioner might say it's invalid, in which case you'll have to fall back on article 9(2)(b) of the GDPR.

How long do we need to keep email communications for? We had intended on having an email retention policy that only keeps emails for six months.

The answer is: it depends. It depends on the purpose for which you're keeping them, because under the GDPR, you're meant to keep them for the amount of time that fits your legitimate purpose and no longer. So if your need is to keep emails just for general commercial purposes, and for records for a short period of time, probably six months is long enough.

If your only need to keep them is to protect yourself from employment litigation, I think you probably need to keep them for about 16 months.

I worked that out on the basis of four months limitation, that's three months to contact Acas and then a month after the Acas certificate, and that once the claim is brought or notified, you might want to have emails dating a year back from that. You might have a year's worth of history before a dismissal or a claim.

Equally, if you want to defend yourself in civil litigation, you probably need to keep seven years' worth of emails. That covers the six year limitation period, plus a year going back. I would always keep emails for seven years.

If a client retains personal records for three years, is it reasonable for an HR consultant to retain them for six years?

Yes, absolutely, because the HR consultant can be sued for negligence for six years, so you need to keep that information for at least six years in order to defend a potential claim of professional negligence. Just make sure you have a privacy notice / retention policy which explains your reasons for keeping the documents for six years.

In the data sharing section of a privacy notice, is it essential that you name the third parties, or can you say 'payroll provider', 'HR provider', etc?

No, you don't need to actually name them. The GDPR makes it absolutely clear that they can be described by category. It can be vague. There's no problem with that at all.

Should we get employees to sign a privacy impact statement in addition to their contract?

No, there's absolutely no need for that at all. The less you give employees to sign, the better. If you're going for the consent route to process their data rather than legitimate interests, or pursuant to a contract, you need them to give consent. That's most commonly done by signature, but they don't need to sign a privacy impact statement. The only reason that you might want them to do it is to prove that they received it. But if you send it to them by email and you've got the email paper trail, then that's done the alternative way.

Do we need explicit consent to respond to reference requests from current or former employees? Or can we incorporate this into a catch-all privacy statement?

If you're in the financial services sector, or the care, or teaching, or other regulated sectors, there is often an obligation to provide references. That means you can rely upon the 'legitimate interest' ground for processing their data.

If not then, technically, you do have to obtain consent. But if they've identified you on their CV as a referee, that establishes consent. If not, you can just deal with that by emailing the employee when you get a reference request and say, "Are you happy for us to provide a reference?" That gives the option for consent, and if they don't reply to it, or if they say no, there's your answer: don't do it.

CONTRACT

Do you have any general advice for the distance a restrictive covenant for competition should cover? The employer is a veterinary practice.

Non-competition clauses are very much out of favour, and have been for more than ten years. The modern approach to enforceable restrictive covenants is to protect customer connections and impede the ex-employee's ability to compete unfairly because of knowledge and influence they acquired when working for you, rather than stopping them competing at all. So non-solicitation and non-dealing clauses are far more likely to be enforced by a court than non-compete clauses.

Having said that, to stand any chance of being upheld, a non-compete clause must be limited to a reasonable distance. That is going to depend on the market. So, if (say) a hairdressing salon or estate agent is based in the centre of London, a two-mile radius is probably going to be too much. But if the salon or agency is in the middle of rural Somerset, a ten-mile radius may be a reasonable distance.

In the context of a veterinary practice much will also depend on the nature of the animals concerned. Cat and dog owners are unlikely to travel a long distance, whereas a specialist vet dealing with farm animals will have a larger catchment area, and hence a larger radius can be justified as requiring protection.

A client outsources their cleaning and has decided they'd like to employ one of the cleaners full-time in a different role. They contacted the cleaning supplier informing them of this, and requested they send someone else in the person's place to do the cleaning role.

The cleaning supplier said 'no' due to the following clause in the person's contract:

"During your time with the company and for a period of 12 months after your engagement with the company has ceased, you agree not to solicit, either directly or indirectly on your account or on behalf of others, any client or customer of the company for business, employment or other such gain."

Is the clause valid?

Maybe – but it doesn't really matter. The clause says that the employee cannot solicit work (or employment) from a company. Here, from what you say, the company did the running; the employee did not solicit a job.

Soliciting has been defined fairly clearly in case law (as it happens, in a case I was in), called *Hydra plc v Anastasi*. It basically means 'to entice or to encourage someone to join you'. Simply having a conversation when it was the other side that approached the person is not soliciting, so the restrictive covenant in the cleaner's contract does not engage; meaning questions of 'reasonableness' don't even arise.

Is it permissible for someone to be engaged as both a zero-hours worker and an employee when they have two distinct roles within an organisation? A superintendent pharmacist has to reduce their hours due to ill health, which we are agreeable to. That's on a normal employment contract. They'd like to do some ad hoc prescription review work when they feel well enough. We'd like to engage them at a lower rate on a zero-hours contract for this.

What you're proposing would be unusual, and it's not something I've ever come across – although there's no legal reason why you can't do it as you describe. But it would be a bit messy, and there's a better way to handle it.

If you've got somebody who's on a fixed, standard, permanent contract, which this person is, albeit with reduced hours because of ill health, the best way to handle it is to simply vary that contract. They're still going to be an employee for the prescription review work, it's just that you don't want to guarantee any hours. So you vary that contract either with just agreement letters or by actually issuing a fresh contract to say:

"We guarantee you X hours a week doing superintendent pharmacy duties. We may also offer you additional hours doing ad hoc prescription review work at a lower rate, £Y per hour. We do not have to offer this, and you do not have to accept it."

That way, it is all dealt with in the same contract. There's no reason to have two separate contracts because that does complicate things, particularly when it comes to issues surrounding redundancy (where, if you've got two separate contracts, you can struggle when it comes to redundancy if you want to end one of them).

I'm working with a car company that has four controllers, three of whom are on a 36-hour week and one of whom is on a 48-hour week. The boss

there wants to equalise them all down to 36 hours. Assuming the fourth employee doesn't agree to come down to 36 hours, what are the employer's options?

It's a straightforward case of imposing a contractual variation, so consulting, and then dismissing and rehiring. The car company will have to establish a good business case for imposing a pay cut, because that's essentially what it is. If they can show a good business case for it, great. If they can't, and if the fourth controller has been employed for over two years, they'll be liable for unfair dismissal.

What issues do we need to bear in mind if someone is hired to report to a director position, but then, through a restructure, it's proposed that they report to a manager instead? Is it a demotion? Is the employee likely to object?

It may be a demotion – more information is needed. But if it is, it's one that you're probably entitled to make if either the terms and conditions say you can change an employee's job description, or change their reporting structure. Any well-drafted contract will say that. It's not nearly as serious a demotion as a cut in pay, and as long as you can show a good sound business reason, you're not going to have any problem.

I wouldn't dismiss and rehire, though, because it's not a situation where you need to worry about them suing you for backpay six years down the line. I'd just tell them they're reporting to the new person, and if they resign and bring a claim for constructive dismissal, you can defend it on its merits. There is no advantage in expressly dismissing them, and thus handing them the 'dismissal' part of 'unfair dismissal' on a plate.

Is there a requirement for collective consultation for sites with more than 20 people for a variation of contract? And if more than 20 at one site refuse to accept a variation, what options do we have? Some employees are getting a small pay increase, some are staying the same, and a small number are having their pay frozen for two years and then a deduction as they're being re-graded.

Under the definition of 'redundancy' for the purpose of collective consultation, if there is a proposal to dismiss (and re-engage) people as part of a process of changing terms and conditions, that falls within a proposed dismissal on grounds of redundancy.

Accordingly, you've got to consult with anybody when you're contemplating dismissing for refusal to accept a change of terms and conditions. If you're changing terms and conditions for more than 20 people, you have to consult collectively.

Therefore, to answer the question, if more than 20 at one site refuse to accept a variation, and you are contemplating dismissing them, you need to consult collectively.

We've received a request from a member of staff who wants to spend part of the year working in one of our overseas offices. This may, or may not, be something we can accommodate. If we can't accommodate it, and they refuse to work in the UK all of the time, and also say they need to work at home, are they in breach of contract?

Once you've followed a reasonable process, you can dismiss. They would be refusing to perform the most fundamental aspect of their work, which is turning up and doing the job.

You would, of course, have to warn them that if they refuse to attend work, they would face a disciplinary charge for gross misconduct, because they would be deliberately refusing to follow their contract. You could hold a disciplinary and give them a right of appeal, but ultimately, without doubt, you would be able to dismiss this person.

There is an exception, of course, which is if their desire to work from home flows from childcare issues or health issues. In that situation, there is the prospect of a discrimination claim, and a more careful analysis is needed.

In relation to the Good Work Plan and the legislative changes that came into force in April 2020, my understanding is that the particulars from Employment Rights Act 1996, s1 need to be included in a single statement, as opposed to referring to other documents. So we can no longer cross-refer to other documents including an employee handbook or collective agreements. Is that correct? What steps should we take?

The changes introduced in 2020 are for written statements of terms. First of all, all workers now come within the scope of the legislation; it's not just employees who will have to be given a statement of particulars. Secondly, everything has to be in one document. Under the old law, you could – as you say – cross-refer to an employee handbook, policies, collective agreements etc.. Now it's all got to be in one document.

There are also a few extra things you have to include. For example, if there's a probationary period, you didn't previously need to include details in a s1 statement. Now you do. If the employee/worker is going to have to pay for any aspect of their own training, you'll need to set out what training they'll have to pay for, and how much it will cost. But the extra sections are limited. It doesn't have to be anything like the level of detail you see in an executive contract, or a big thick policy.

From a risk and litigation perspective, an employee or worker can bring a claim for a statement of written particulars of employment under section 11 of the *Employment Rights Act*. The tribunal can then make a declaration as to what the correct terms are, but two or four weeks' pay can only be awarded as compensation if there is another successful claim that's brought, so it's a piggyback claim.

GRIEVANCES AND DISCIPLINARIES

A manager who suffers from stress, anxiety and depression raised a grievance against one of their team alleging bullying. The bullying behaviour included badmouthing the manager to others and mild swearing (e.g. "He is an arse").

Several of the allegations were upheld, and the investigating officer recommended that the bullying be dealt with by a formal disciplinary process.

However, the area manager wants to deal with the matter informally instead. HR is worried that the area manager is not taking the matter seriously enough and that the stress being caused may continue. How should we proceed?

The bullying behaviour all sounds pretty minor, and the sort of thing that employees say about their manager all the time, although I do understand the cumulative effect of all of this can be quite significant.

The question is whether, if there is no disciplinary outcome as a result of the grievance findings, the company has acted in a way that is likely to destroy or seriously damage the employment relationship between the company and the manager – and I think it probably will. Of course, it's a defence to a constructive dismissal claim if the company has good cause, but I don't think the area manager not taking things seriously is sufficient.

So, assuming the manager has worked for the company for two years, I think they would have a claim for constructive dismissal if something's not done formally about the bullying, because they have invoked a formal process. I don't think the subordinate team member needs to be dismissed; I think a verbal warning would be more than adequate given the nature of the bullying. "He is an arse" is relatively minor, but there should be some form of formal response.

However, a sensible middle ground is sending a 'letter of concern'. Without holding the disciplinary process, write a letter of concern to the employee saying, "This has been placed in your file and we don't want to see any similar behaviour or it will result in a disciplinary process." That will probably satisfy the manager who lodged the grievance, and that's what I would do in this position.

Is the recording of disciplinary meetings covered by the GDPR? We have a situation where a union representative who's subject to a disciplinary hearing, is recording the meetings without the consent of the individuals in attendance. I personally do not believe meetings should be recorded unless all parties are in agreement and a copy of the agreement is given to all parties at the end of the meeting. Any thoughts on the subject?

This raises lots of different issues. First of all, I disagree that you (or the employee) should be requesting consent, because it's those who are likely to create erroneous notes, mis-recollect meetings or lie about what happened in meetings, that would be unlikely to consent to the recording of meetings. They're also the very people who create a situation where there is the most need to record the meetings.

I think that if an employee asks to record the meetings, the answer should always be, "Yes, that's fine." Because otherwise, tribunals may think, "What's the employer trying to hide here? Why don't they want a clear, accurate record of what happened at that meeting? It must be because they want there to be an inaccurate record, that they want to finesse the record. They must want the notes to reveal only what they want them to show after the event." So, if an employee asked to record a meeting, I would say 'yes' every single time. By all means take your own recording as well, in case there is doubt about the accuracy or completeness of the employee's recording, but never refuse permission.

I think the GDPR issue is actually a non-issue because (if the employee is recording) the employer would not be the data controller in that situation; rather, the employee would. But as long as everyone has been informed, you can justify the recording as being legitimate processing for the purpose of acting pursuant to an employment contract. If the employee is recording the meeting, the employee is the data controller.

In a disciplinary, if an employee wants to be accompanied by a representative from a trade union that is not recognised by the business, can you stop them from coming?

No. Recognition is about collective bargaining, not disciplinaries and grievances. You don't need to recognise the trade union for the representative to have the right to attend.

Under the Employment Relations Act 1999, if they're employed or certified by a trade union –

which would include a shop steward or anybody appropriate who the union has reasonably certified in writing as having experience of or having received training in acting as a companion at disciplinary or grievance hearings – they are legally permitted to attend the meeting (and you have an obligation to postpone the meeting for up to five days to allow them to attend). So even if you don't recognise the union, you still have to let the union representative attend.

If you have concerns about a Trade Union, check their status here: https://www.gov.uk/government/publications/public-list-of-active-trade-unions-official-list-and-schedule

---

If a trade union representative wants to cross-examine a witness in a disciplinary hearing, are you obliged to let them?

No. There is no obligation to allow a witness to be cross-examined by an employee during a disciplinary hearing. The law is crystal clear on that. You're the employer, you're the person who can and should be doing it.

What you do have an obligation to do is to put any questions to that witness, but you don't need to allow the employee or the trade union representative to do it. So you can ask them for the list of questions that they want you to ask the witness, and you can then ask the witness. It's a good idea to make sure that the conversation is carefully noted or recorded.

Following *Talon Engineering v Smith*, can you give any guidance as to how long we should delay a disciplinary hearing if a trade union representative is unavailable?

I can tell you exactly how much extra time should be allowed: a 'reasonable amount'. Five days is the legal minimum, but assuming the individual you're likely to dismiss has more than two years' employment at your company, you should allow longer unless you are confident you can persuade a tribunal there is a good reason for you not allowing longer (and that won't be easy).

If there is a credible reason why the trade union representative cannot be there, and they're not messing around, you have got to allow a reasonable period for them to attend. If we are talking a week, or a 10-day delay, it is likely to be unreasonable not to allow that. If it's two to three weeks, it's greyer. As you get beyond three weeks, it will generally be reasonable to refuse. Large unions should have the capacity to send an alternative representative to avoid causing an undue delay, although they may be reluctant to do so as continuity of representation can be important.

An employee used their mobile phone while driving. It was witnessed by a fellow employee, but the police were not involved. The employee denies it. How can this be dealt with under sanctions? Are we allowed to believe one employee over another?

Yes, you absolutely can. In fact, isn't that the very essence of most disciplinary proceedings? You've got to decide who you believe. So, you have a meeting and make up your mind. If you believe the employee making the allegation, that leads to a finding of guilt. If you don't believe the employee making the allegation, and you believe the employee who's been accused, then there is no finding of guilt.

Remember the *Burchell* test: you've got to conduct a reasonable investigation and have an honest belief on reasonable grounds. The fact that you've got somebody who saw the individual using a mobile phone while driving is a reasonable ground for believing that the accused employee was using a mobile phone while driving, unless there is credible reason to believe that employee was mistaken or making it up.

If an employee is suspended due to safeguarding concerns in an adult social care situation and

the police are investigating, is there anything the employer can do while the employee is suspended, as they are currently on full pay?

There are three things the employer can do:

1. suck it up and carry on paying. That is the most cautious thing to do.

2. do their own investigation, separate from the police investigation. It'll take a few weeks, but tribunals expect that to be done. Then, if the employer finds something proven, they can dismiss. Remember: the employer only needs to have reasonable grounds for their belief in guilt after reasonable investigation. They don't need to prove beyond reasonable doubt. So even if the police were to end up finding something unproven, an employer is still allowed to find it proven.

3. this won't help this time around, but it will help next time around: amend the contracts of employment so that they state that if somebody is on suspension because of safeguarding concerns for, say, more than four weeks, then no salary is payable. However, that requires a contract amendment and clearly that is not going to work for this employee, unless they agree to it as an alternative to dismissal, once you've embarked on a formal dismissal process.

HOLIDAY PAY

Do employees continue to accrue holiday during a sabbatical?

During a sabbatical there will normally be a contract of employment in place, unless it has been terminated. The employees therefore earn 5.6 weeks' paid holiday, and are entitled to claim the money. Of course, if they don't use it during the relevant holiday year, then (unless the contract allows carry-over of holiday) they lose the right to claim it.

Do voluntary overtime or overnight allowance payments count towards holiday pay?

Yes, as long as they're regular and predictable, i.e. they're part of 'normal remuneration'. If the worker does overtime or overnights once in a blue moon, then they won't. The recent Court of Appeal case, *Flowers v East of England Ambulance Trust*, dealt with this issue.

When exiting an employee via a settlement agreement, does the pay in lieu of notice payment have the same terms as in a redundancy situation? For example, does the employee continue to accrue annual leave during the period of notice, even though there's an agreed exit date.

That is going to depend on the phrasing of the settlement agreement. The employee accrues annual leave up to their effective date of termination.

So, if they have a payment in lieu of notice where, let's say, their last day of work is going to be 1 May, and you'll pay them three months' salary in respect of May, June and July (which they're not going to work), and their effective date of termination is 1 May, then they don't get holiday for the May, June and July because the effective date of termination is 1 May.

However, if the settlement agreement is phrased, "Your employment is going to end on 31 July, but you don't need to come into work; we'll pay you in lieu of that," then the effective date of termination will be 31 July, and they will get their holiday entitlement for May, June and July. It really is just a matter of phrasing.

SICKNESS ABSENCE

What should we pay an employee during their notice period, if they're signed off sick? Normal pay? Or statutory sick pay?

This is complicated. It's governed by sections 87-91 of the Employment Rights Act 1996. I'm going to have to simplify it a little, and even on a simplified basis, it's a bit complex. There are two possibilities, which depend on the length of both the employee's contractual and statutory notice periods.

If the contractual notice period is the same as the statutory notice period, or up to a week more, you have to pay them their normal basic pay (but not extras, such as voluntary overtime they might have earned). So if somebody who has worked for four years has a one month notice period in their contract, they will be entitled to normal pay during their notice. That's because their contractual notice period (one month) is less than a week more than their statutory notice period (four weeks). Complicated, right?

By contrast, if the contractual notice period is more than a week over their statutory minimum notice period, they are not entitled to normal pay during their notice period – just SSP (if it has not already run out). And before you ask; I've got no idea why this is.

Depending on timings, you may be able to require an employee to take part of their paid annual leave during their notice period – which is likely to reduce the overall cost of termination.

An employee has been off sick following a couple of small operations. The employee's GP has said they're fit to return to work, but the work involves heavy lifting and we're a bit worried. Would you recommend making a referral to occupational health?

If the employee is certified by their GP as fit to return to work, and they want to return, that's pretty much the end of it. It's very difficult to turn around and say, "actually, we don't think you're fit to work," unless there is a credible, compelling reason to do so.

I wouldn't worry about seeking a report from occupational health, because the employee has said they are fit to work and they've got medical evidence corroborating they're fit to work. You can only act on the information received.

The only exception might be if you had a credible reason to think that the employee *wasn't fit* to return to work, and that the GP was just going along with what the employee asked them to put in a fit note. That might be the case, for example, if the fitness to return coincided with the ending of company sick pay, and the employee had previously been saying they remained unfit.

Leaving that aside, it's easy to be too risk averse, and this doesn't strike me as a high-risk issue. If you're really, really worried, then get the occupational health report: but you've got to continue paying the employee full pay while you're getting that report. You can't keep them on statutory sick pay if they've been certified as fit to return to work.

I've got someone who's taken an awful lot of sick leave while on probation. In their first three months, they were off for 17 days with Irritable Bowel Syndrome. Their line manager is reluctant to do very much. The trouble is, the person goes off sick, doesn't contact us, and then says: "Sorry,

I was staying at my parents' and they don't have broadband." So they're effectively AWOL.

My view is that we need to get an assessment and then, potentially, there could be a disciplinary issue. Really, if they're behaving like this on probation it's not going to get any better. What's your view?

You just take a normal decision at the end of the probationary period. I suppose, theoretically, IBS could be a disability if it's sufficiently serious that they have to rush off to the toilet more frequently than people who don't suffer from IBS, as a result of which they're impaired in going to (e.g.) the cinema, or engaging in other normal day-to-day activities.

But you're dealing with something related to a disability here. You're not dismissing them *because* they've got IBS, you're dismissing them because they've got an appalling attendance record and they're in their probationary period.

I wouldn't have thought you would have much difficulty justifying that under the *Equality Act 2010*. You have to make reasonable adjustments, but reasonable adjustments will, at most, extend your trigger dates and the level of absence you're prepared to tolerate. It doesn't extend to saying: "You don't have to come to work that often, because we understand you want to stay at home, and you need to stay at home." Plus there are also conduct issues here. Their parents may not have broadband, but surely they have a telephone? The fact they go AWOL and don't comply with basic sickness notification requirements is, itself, enough of a reason to end their contract during the probationary period.

If a manager shares the reason for an employee's sickness absence with other employees, could that be a potential breach of contract (giving rise to a constructive dismissal)? Colleagues have been told the employee is 'off with stress', and the employee has now raised a grievance.

That's a tough one. It's certainly a breach of confidentiality, but it's reasonably low level (I'd take a very different view if a manager told somebody that an employee was off with, say, gonorrhea).

If the employee has specifically asked for their reason to be kept confidential, or they're in a role where a reputation for suffering from stress might damage their professional standing, then it probably will amount to a breach of trust and confidence. In other situations, probably not – but I could see different tribunals reaching different conclusions on this.

What you *should* do is investigate the grievance promptly (and you'll doubtless find it proven), and then you should put the manager through a disciplinary process – and they deserve one because they should know better. A low-level disciplinary sanction will normally be sufficient; I'd be happy with a verbal warning if it's a first offence.

Is an employer obliged to share with an individual who's the subject of an occupational health referral the specific questions that we wish to ask?

Yes and no. Mostly yes.

You don't have to send them a copy in advance, or at the same time you write to the occupational health practitioner.

But they are entitled to insist on seeing a copy of the medical report before it is sent to you, and that medical report will inevitably include the questions you've asked (assuming the occupational health expert has answered them).

Also, if they lodge a subject access request, they will be entitled to see the questions, and if they bring tribunal proceedings, they will get copies of the correspondence during disclosure.

So, as I said, yes and no – but mostly yes.

An employee with two years' service has been absent for six months. They're receiving statutory sick pay. Occupational health say the employee has got long-term mental health problems and is being investigated for fibromyalgia. Our intention is to refer the employee back to occupational health in two months, after which we will make a decision on whether or not to continue their employment. The employee is ignoring our request for a meeting to discuss the occupational health report. If they refuse to engage in any other form of communication at this stage, what do you recommend?

I think you're doing everything right at the moment. If they're refusing to engage with the report, I'm not even sure I'd bother with referring them back in two months, unless the occupational health report says you should do so. If the occupational health report says that the employee is not likely to be returning to work in the foreseeable future, and they're refusing to engage with you, I think you can go straight to dismissal and just write a letter saying, "We've received this report from occupational health. It looks like you're not returning to work in the reasonably foreseeable future. We've tried to engage with you but you're not responding. In light of the medical evidence and our difficulties speaking with you, we are considering whether your employment can realistically continue. To that end, please would you attend a meeting on [date], at which we want to discuss the next steps. If you do not contact us (for example to rearrange) or attend, we are likely to take the decision to dismiss you at that meeting. Any dismissal will be with notice."

If the occupational health report actually states you should review again in two months, then that's different. I think you're probably at a more advanced stage in this process than you think you are. And I also think you are on stronger ground than you think.

Where does an employer stand in terms of payment if they send an unwell employee home? Employee X turns up for work, they're limping, and they're a manual worker. The manager sends them home as they don't think the employee can work safely. Do we have to pay them their normal salary, or follow the SSP system?

As always, the answer is that it depends. They have a contractual right to payment if they're ready, willing and able to work. They're clearly *willing* to work, because they've turned up to work, albeit limping. They're ready to work, because they're physically there. The question is: are they *able* to work?

If they are not capable of doing the job despite the fact they've turned up, then they're not ready, willing and able to work. Therefore, they can be sent home, because they haven't presented themselves in a way that they're meant to: ready, willing and able. In that circumstance there's no obligation to pay them salary.

But if they *are* able to work (even if they're not working at 100% capacity; if they're fundamentally able to do much of the job) then they're entitled to their salary. If you choose to send them home, they're still entitled to their salary. If an employee is a manual worker, I'm not sure a limp is necessarily fatal to them doing their job. If you don't pay them their salary yet they are objectively 'able' to work, then they will have a claim against you for unlawful deductions from wages. If they've worked for more than two years, they will also have a constructive dismissal claim.

The risk, here, is yours. If you are sued for the backpay, you will have to prove that the individual was unable to work despite them turning up and being willing to do so. And it's not a very attractive argument to run, particularly if you don't have any medical evidence to support it.

An employee went off sick and was signed off by their GP for a month. The employee then decided they wanted to be treated in Poland, so they went

and left the country. We've had a Polish doctor's note from the employee, and the employee has emailed to say they'll be back in the UK once the Polish doctor allows it. How do we deal with an absent employee who is abroad?

I am assuming here that there is no reason to doubt the authenticity of the Polish doctor's note. You're not going to be able to get the employee to come and see occupational health. There's no harm in asking, but if the employee doesn't do it, you can't do anything about it. Any tribunal will say that it is an unreasonable instruction to require the employee to travel from Poland to the UK to see a doctor of your choice.

So, your options are these: find a Polish occupational health consultant (that may not be easy, as it's hard enough to find someone who will do a good job in the UK, let alone overseas), or try putting questions to the Polish doctor.

However, I'm sceptical about how things will come across in translation and the extent to which an overseas medic would be frank with a UK employer. A lot of occupational health consultations don't require face-to-face meetings, so you could arrange a Skype or phone consultation.

Failing that, you probably need to just wait and see what happens. If the employee doesn't return within, say, six months, at that point you can start to engage in absence management. At that point you can say, 'We now want absence management meetings. It's your choice whether you attend or not (and we can do it by Zoom or by telephone). But if you don't attend, we'll take a decision in your absence.'

DISCRIMINATION

I s the protection against discrimination on the grounds of religious belief based on what the requirements of the religion are, or is it based on the individual's own beliefs? For example, some Christians believe they should wear a crucifix, but not all do.

Tribunals don't examine how core a belief is within the spectrum of religious observance. There's a case on this, *Eweida and others v British Airways plc.* It's the case of the British Airways check-in operator who wore a small crucifix around her neck, in breach of British Airways' dress code (which banned visible jewellery). The court said, very clearly, that even though many Christians do not believe it's necessary to wear a crucifix, some do, and that attracts religious protection.

The Equality and Human Rights Commission Code of Practice says:

"A person does not have to prove that the manifestation of their religion or belief is a core component of the religion they follow. It may be a means by which they choose to express their adherence to their religious belief."

We are a small private bank in the UK with Middle Eastern clients. Can we safely include speaking Arabic as a requirement for members of our front office team?

The answer to that is – as so often is the case – it depends.

Requiring fluency in Arabic is potentially indirect discrimination on grounds of both nationality and race. But like all forms of indirect discrimination, it can be justified if requiring front-office employees to speak Arabic is a proportionate means of achieving a legitimate aim.

There is no doubt that having Arabic speakers to service predominately Middle Eastern clients is a legitimate aim. Whether or not requiring *everyone* to speak Arabic is a proportionate means is where I think there may be a potential difficulty.

If all the bank's clients only speak Arabic, then I can understand that all front office staff need to speak Arabic. But if it's only a *proportion* of the clients that speak Arabic, and most of those Arabic speakers also speak fluent English, then requiring *everyone* to speak Arabic may be overkill. You would need to ensure that there is cover of at least one person who speaks Arabic on duty at any one time – and that would involve examining the practicability of appropriate rotas and cover.

An employee started work with us six months ago. Throughout their probation period, there were lots of last-minute dramas, requiring them to take annual leave at short notice. We then found out that their child and partner have mental health issues, and that caused them to take time off. The employee takes many personal calls in the day and has had some sickness absence.

We basically said to the employee, "You need to improve your attendance, and nip the personal calls in the bud." The employee did pass their probation as the manager didn't want to extend it or fail the employee for commercial reasons. This employee has now had about five weeks off with low mood and depression. They say it's the first time that they have experienced this. The employee is back at work and is still not great. They're late, they're not keeping in touch, they're having doctor's appointments and only telling us two minutes before that they've got to go.

If we look to dismiss, what is the risk from a discrimination perspective?

First, due to the short length of service, there is no risk of an unfair dismissal claim, because the employee hasn't got two years' employment.

However, there are two potential discrimination issues arising. First of all, there is associative discrimination, and second, there's discrimination against the employee. If they're having problems because their partner and child are disabled, that gives rise to a risk of associated disability discrimination claims. But it sounds as though the employee has been taking more time off than could reasonably be expected to be supported by the business, to look after their partner and child. I don't think there's a major risk there.

In terms of the employee's absence, and their potential disability discrimination claim, there's a very real chance that the employee is actually not disabled because of the 12-month rule (i.e. that their condition has to be likely to last more than 12 months).

So, unless the employee's condition is likely to last more than 12 months, they're not disabled and you don't have to worry about the *Equality Act.* For that reason it is probably better to act sooner, rather than sit on it for a while, because if you sit on it for another six months, the employee will have built up their 12 months, and they will probably qualify as disabled.

I think it is quite a low-risk strategy to dismiss at this point, because the employee's attendance record is abject. But much more significant is the problem with the employee just going to medical appointments without telling you about them first. That's going to be quite difficult for the employee to explain away as related to their disability. It's just poor communication on their part.

There is always some risk in this sort of situation, but in this case, I think it's a relatively low-risk claim, and the risk would likely increase as time passes. So if you're willing to accept a little bit of risk, I'd dismiss now, and not wait and see what happens in three months' time.

DISMISSAL

A settlement agreement provides for a termination payment of £8,000. It is conditional on the employee abiding by post-termination restrictive covenants. Is it detrimental to the employer to put a nominal value of, say, £50 of the £8,000 against the restrictive covenant condition, in order to protect the employee against the risk of HMRC claiming tax on the whole ex-gratia payment?

Yes, it is detrimental. HMRC rules provide that the first £30,000 of termination payments are tax free (after post-employment notice pay has been taken account of). But there are exceptions to that. One of the exceptions is where a payment is in respect of restrictive covenants. Those payments (so the £50 in this case) *is* taxable.

In order to ensure a restrictive covenant in a settlement agreement is enforceable, the law states you should allocate a sensible commercial payment towards them.

If you make a nominal payment, whether it's £1 or £50, it gives a court the opportunity to say that the employer placed so little weight on these covenants that they can't be that important. If they're not as important, they're not reasonably necessary for the protection of the business, therefore not enforceable. It gives the Judge a way around enforcing them if they're looking for a reason not to do so.

Ultimately, it's just a balancing act. There is no magic answer here. You may have to attribute more money (which then becomes taxable). £1,000 is a reasonably safe amount.

As part of cost-saving measures, our two directors have decided that they and the two senior managers should reduce their pay by 15%. One of the managers is refusing. Is it reasonable to dismiss the manager for some other substantial reason?

Yes, provided you are confident you can persuade a tribunal that the business needs to make the cuts in order to secure its future. It can't just be a way of cutting the pay of two senior managers by directors who have a substantial remuneration, or draw the bulk of the income via dividends, meaning that the 15% cut has less impact on them. And it can't just be for show, to make it look like they're doing something reasonable.

If you can establish that, and also establish that there are no other measures that can reasonably be taken, then any dismissal is likely to be fair for 'some other substantial reason'.

An alternative which I prefer, rather than a salary cut, is a salary deferral. So instead of cutting the manager's pay by 15%, propose that 15% of the salary is deferred until the business re-establishes a certain level of profitability (assuming the manager is still in employment).

If an employee with less than two years' service is dismissed and subsequently issues a discrimination claim in the tribunal, does the procedure that was followed have a bearing on any award that's made?

Yes, it does, because when there's a dismissal situation, the Acas Code applies, even if the employee has less than two years' service.

Of course, if they have less than two years' service, they cannot claim unfair dismissal - so to that extent, the Acas Code is irrelevant. But in a discrimination claim, if you have not complied with the Acas Code, there can be an uplift of up to 25% in the compensatory award. Discrimination cases, of course, involve potentially bigger awards, so unless you are confident they have no protected characteristics or have no real chance of arguing the dismissal was connected with a protected characteristic, it is prudent to comply with the Code.

A client has dismissed an employee who moved from Germany to London about a year ago. It now transpires that the employee is claiming continuity of service because they previously worked for an employer in Germany for four years, then moved to our client's company in London. Both companies are ultimately controlled by the same parent. The two companies are associated employers. What is the position on continuity when there's an overseas associated employer?

If they're associated employers, continuity doesn't get broken, it just continues in the normal way. The fact that the first employer was based overseas doesn't actually matter; the *Employment Rights Act 1996* does not limit the rules on continuity to time spent working within Great Britain.

International conflict of laws, which is all about which country's laws should be enforced, says that British employment law – unfair dismissal law – won't apply unless the individual works in Great Britain or has a very strong connection with Britain. For example, if they're an expat, a diplomat or a peripatetic employee (such as a pilot flying in and out of Heathrow), etc.

But for continuity purposes, if they're working for an associated employer overseas, they will accrue continuity. I think you're going to struggle here. I can see some arguments that would work for you and could be run if you're instructed to defend this at all costs. But ultimately, I think the ex-employee is correct and will have four years' continuity of service.

Are there any issues with insisting an employee takes accrued holiday leave within their notice period when they're being dismissed on ill-health grounds? The company handbook says that employees are normally required to use outstanding leave before the end of their notice period. They've got 18 days' holiday. They can be given the necessary notice under the Working Time Regulations. Can we require them to take their holiday?

Yes and no. You can give the employee notice under the *Working Time Regulations* to take their 18 days' holiday during the eight weeks' notice. That's fairly straightforward.

But there are European cases that came into force several years ago that say that if somebody is ill while on holiday, they have the absolute right to elect to treat that period as sick, not holiday. That means that if the employee knows this (most people don't) they may respond: "Actually, no. I'm sick. Here's my sick note. And of course, you're dismissing me for long-term sickness. I'm electing to take it as sick, not holiday." The employee would then be entitled to get their 18 days' holiday pay on termination.

But the chances are they're not going to do that. And if they do, well, the worst-case scenario is that you have to pay them the holiday that you would've paid them anyway if you hadn't tried to make them take it as part of their notice.

If there are a number of people in a work environment who feel uncomfortable with an employee returning to work due to very erratic behaviour, threats of violence, etc., would we be able to dismiss that employee for some other substantial reason?

Normally, yes. Concerns by colleagues are an absolute classic reason for dismissal for some other substantial reason.

However, there are some caveats.

First, if the employee has mental health issues which are serious enough to amount to a disability, and which are causing their erratic behaviour, then they may have a claim for dismissal for a reason associated with their disability under the *Equality*

Act 2010. You can justify dismissal if you can show that dismissing the employee is a proportionate means of achieving a legitimate business aim, which would be a calm, pleasant work environment. But there is inevitably litigation risk.

Second, if the employee is unpopular because they've whistleblown – even if that reason has been concealed from you by the staff who are complaining – you might be at risk of a whistleblowing claim.

Finally (assuming the employee has two years' employment), you still have to show that you took reasonable steps to try to repair relationships, and that you tried to get people to understand the employee's position but it just proved to be impossible.

An employee went off sick with sciatica. Just as they were due to return to work, they had a heart attack and they were off for a further four months. The employee returned to work for two months and has now been diagnosed with cancer (no prognosis yet). The employee is currently off work again on SSP. Their job involves a lot of travel, but they need to be at home regularly for hospital appointments.

The continued absence is proving a real problem. Can we justify dismissal?

The employee is plainly disabled; cancer is deemed to be a disability. You've got to make reasonable adjustments. I find it hard to see why you would need to dismiss them. Surely the business can just hire somebody to fill the employee's role and tell them that if they want to come back in due course, they can.

There's no way that the employee having to stay at home to be near the hospital for tests could justify dismissal. You would simply be dismissing for a reason associated with the cancer, and you would struggle to justify the dismissal. Apart from the odd day that I accept the employee will need for check-ups, their previous illnesses are self-contained; they're in the past.

So what you're really trying to justify here is a dismissal two weeks after a cancer diagnosis without any clear prognosis, no knowledge of how long the employee is likely to be off or whether they're likely to be returning to work at all. It's just too soon to dismiss and be safe.

Of course, the sad reality is that if you do dismiss and the employee brings a claim for unfair dismissal and disability discrimination, by the time you get to a tribunal, nine or 12 months down the line, it might have become obvious that they would never have returned to work. But you can't judge the chances of that at the moment; it's too early. And that's why a tribunal would say it's too early to dismiss, precisely because you can't judge the chances of that.

It might just be a situation where you sit down and have a settlement discussion with the employee, but I think a dismissal now would involve a very high level of risk. At the moment, you haven't got medical evidence justifying dismissal. You've got to get medical evidence with a clear prognosis from the employee's treating doctor. If the doctor won't give you a clear prognosis, then maybe three or four months down the line you can look at dismissing, unless a clear prognosis saying the employee will return to work in the reasonable future can be produced. But you're nowhere close at the moment. And – on a human level – just pause and think: do you really want to be that employer?

One of my clients has got a cleaner who cleans at odd hours in the evening, ten hours a week. The cleaner has been signed off sick for a couple of weeks. However, we know that they are actually working for another company doing cleaning. The client wants to dismiss, but the cleaner has worked for more than two years. How should we progress?

It is possible, of course, that the cleaner has some sort of medical condition that means they can only work a limited number of hours, and they are fulfilling another contract they already had – just not yours. You can't rule that out. If that's the case, then you would expect the cleaner to provide medical evidence saying exactly that.

I would call the cleaner in for a disciplinary meeting. The letter should make it very clear what the allegations are:

"You've sent us a fit note saying you can't work for us; however, it has come to our attention that you may be working for another company [state name if known]. If that is right, and unless there is a good explanation for it, we regard this as potential gross misconduct. Please return to work immediately if you are well enough to do so. If you are not, we will look into whether you are genuinely ill or whether - as our information suggests - you are moonlighting."

Three weeks ago, an employee was told that they were going to be put through a performance management process. They resigned. Two days before the end of their notice period they said, "I never wanted to resign, it was just an emotional reaction." Where does that leave us in terms of whether we allow the employee to rescind their resignation or not?

They cannot retract their resignation. There is case law that says that if somebody resigns in the heat of the moment, and they retract their resignation within a reasonable period, an employer should allow them to retract. But a 'reasonable period' in the case law has been said to be one or two days, or possibly over a weekend.

Three weeks falls way outside that period, so there is nothing to worry about. If they resigned, the tribunal will accept that resignation. There is no obligation on the employer to allow this person to come back. You can take the resignation at face value.

An employee has resigned, and during their notice period, they are suspended due to conduct issues. The employee now believes that their resignation no longer stands and that they can remain employed on full pay. I have said no as their resignation was accepted prior to the suspension. Where do we stand?

The resignation remains effective. The employee is suspended during their period of notice, but once their notice has expired, they are no longer employed. It is now a matter of whether you want to carry on with the disciplinary.

I wouldn't bother, frankly, unless you think there is a chance that the employee may claim constructive dismissal and say that they resigned because of a breach of contract by the employer. In that case, you might want to have the disciplinary process as a fall back to argue that if they hadn't resigned, they would have been dismissed anyway.

We've got an employee who is currently awaiting trial for a very serious criminal offence. If they are convicted, they are likely to be jailed for several years. Can we dismiss for some other substantial reason?

If the employee is convicted, you have a strong argument that the contract of employment is frustrated. You shouldn't normally rely on frustration for long-term sickness dismissals, but it's still valid to use in situations involving imprisonment if it's a long sentence. A six-month sentence would not be long enough, but if someone's going to get at least several years, the contract is probably frustrated.

The impact of the contract being frustrated is that no notice pay will be due. Assuming that there is something in your disciplinary policy about bringing your organisation into disrepute, if the employee has been linked with your organisation in the press, then, in any event, you can dismiss them for gross misconduct for bringing the organisation into disrepute.

Otherwise, notice pay is due if the contract is not frustrated. So, what I would do is, if or when the employee is convicted, write a letter saying: *"Your employment is terminated on the grounds of frustration because you've been imprisoned for X years. But if we're wrong about that, we are dismissing you without notice for some other substantial reason due to your conviction and long-term imprisonment."* That's all it needs.

We are a charity and we have an employee who has worked for us for eight months as a carer. They didn't turn up for several shifts without contact, then went AWOL for three weeks.

We wrote a letter basically saying, "If we don't hear from you within two weeks, we'll assume that you've resigned."

The employee then got in touch and said that they had been suffering from anxiety, which is corroborated by a GP report obtained by the company. There was no mention of a disability. We have made adjustments, reducing their hours and adjusting shifts, etc., but now the employee has gone AWOL again. Can we safely dismiss?

There is a risk that the employee is disabled. The threshold is fairly low, and if the anxiety is sufficient to stop the employee working, it could well cross that threshold.

If they are, indeed, disabled, you need to show you have attempted reasonable adjustments yet they have proven insufficient, and you can't continue to employ them.

Where somebody is a carer for charity, they need to turn up to work, much more so than if they're a call centre operator in a big call centre with 200 people doing the same thing. Carers have to turn up to work. You've given the employee lots of chances. You've reduced hours, you've adjusted shifts and you've bent over backwards to allow them to stay – yet they're still not turning up to work.

Assuming that the employee is not disabled, you could just dismiss them with a week's notice for failing to attend work. There's no risk of unfair dismissal there because they haven't got their two years' service.

But even if they are disabled, I think the chances of them succeeding in a disability discrimination claim – given the nature of the work and the steps you've taken – is low. So dismissal is a commercially acceptable risk.

If an employee is detained indefinitely without charge in a different country, how long is considered reasonable to hold their role open before dismissing them? Would the dismissal be for 'some other substantial reason', or something different?

First of all, the employment contract is arguably frustrated. Frustration is something that you only rely on as a fallback when everything else has gone wrong, but there's no reason not to mention it in a letter if you don't want to pay notice, because the worst case scenario is you get sued and have to pay the notice you would have voluntarily paid anyway.

The first thing I would do is say that the contract's frustrated and have a contemporaneous note of that. As the employee is being held indefinitely without charge, I think there is a decent chance a tribunal would accept that after three to six months the contract is frustrated, depending on the seniority of the role and what the individual does. If someone is a relatively low-level worker and there's lots of people doing their job, you probably have to wait longer. If it's the chief executive officer or the chief financial officer of a FTSE 100 company, you'd be able to justify waiting less time.

If you don't go down the frustration route, and you want to dismiss, yes, it is 'some other substantial reason' for dismissal. You'd need to go through a theoretical process of saying, "We're going to have a meeting; we appreciate you can't attend, but if we can contact you, if you're picking up emails, you can try making submissions to us by email, however unlikely that may be."

As long as you show that you've gone through a process of giving them every chance you can – you can even invite their relatives to make submissions, or if they're a member of a union, get the union to make submissions on their behalf – then it's a dismissal for some other substantial reason, and you'd be incredibly unlucky for that to be held subsequently to be unfair.

MISCELLANEOUS

An employee has gone off sick, leaving their Facebook account logged in on their work computer. The employer has looked at the employee's Facebook account and seen derogatory messages about the company. To what extent is it acceptable for the employer to look at the employee's Facebook account?

The employer can look at it. Technically, it is regarded as poor practice to do so. It is arguably a breach of privacy, but it is admissible in an employment tribunal, without a shadow of a doubt. A tribunal will say, "That's really naughty; you shouldn't have looked at that. But now let's read the evidence." It's a little more complex if it's a public sector employer, but for private small and medium-sized enterprises (SMEs), there is no doubt the employer can rely on it and the evidence is admissible.

So, you can rely on that as an allegation of gross misconduct in a disciplinary hearing. The allegation would be bringing the company into disrepute by posting negative comments on Facebook. Investigate fully and if you find it proven, then you can dismiss for gross misconduct.

What responsibility does an employer have if they learn that their 17-year-old apprentice is drinking alcohol and talking about getting drunk on a night out?

Normally, none. I'm assuming this is in their personal time, not work time, and they're not doing (for example) security work at night for the employer, in which case they might be drunk on duty.

There are two exceptions:

1. particular jobs requiring complete sobriety the next day (aeroplane pilot being the most extreme example, although there aren't many 17 year old pilots)

2. where the drunkenness occurs at an office party, or some similar organised or semi-official works event. In that situation, if the 17 year old does anything improper, the employer may be vicariously liable.

Other than those two situations, the employer is not responsible for the 17 year old; the employer's duty of care doesn't extend that far. Rhetorically, what is the employer expected to do to avoid breaching their duty? Do they take the person to one side and say, "Naughty, naughty, don't do that"? It's unlikely to have very much effect.

Where a company offers enhanced maternity pay (one year's full pay) what happens if an employee on maternity leave is made redundant? Will they still get the full year's pay, or will that end on the effective date of termination?

If the person is made redundant, they continue to get their statutory maternity pay (SMP). If they are entitled to enhanced maternity pay, then, as a matter of contract law or statute, they are not entitled to it once they've passed the effective date of termination. A word of caution: if they've been selected for redundancy for the purpose of preventing them from getting the enhanced pay, then that's clearly going to be sex discrimination.

Assuming that this is a genuine redundancy situation, the employee will continue to get their SMP, but they won't get the enhanced element of it unless the contract says they will. Inevitably, the contract will be silent on the point, which means they're not entitled to the enhanced rate.

When taking shared parental leave, can there be a gap between one partner and the other taking the leave? When both return to work, does shared parental leave cease, or can they take a period at any time during the fifty weeks?

They can both return to work. They can both take different times off. There can be gaps. It won't affect their entitlement to shared parental leave, and that is because regulation 7 of the *Shared Parental Leave Regulations* allows 'discontinuous' periods of leave. Shared parental leave may be taken as one continuous period or in discontinuous periods.

If an employee makes a racist remark on their personal Facebook account outside of working hours, would the employer be liable for any offence caused towards their employees?

Probably not if it's a remark made on a personal account, outside of working hours, from home. That is, unless it's in some way associated with work, in which case there might be vicarious liability. So, if it was, for example, a remark made from home on a Facebook account used to organise a work party, then the employer may be liable for that. But short of that, no.

But of course, the fact that they're making racist remarks on their personal Facebook account is important and serious, nevertheless. If the employee's Facebook account identifies them as an employee of your company, screenshot the comment before it gets taken off. In that situation, you might want to think about disciplinary proceedings because they are potentially bringing your company into disrepute.

In addition, a failure to take action to discipline or dismiss that employee may mean, in a future discrimination claim, you would be unable to rely on the statutory defence (i.e. that you've taken all reasonable steps to prevent the type of discrimination complained of). The statutory defence is a powerful defence, although difficult to invoke successfully, which means an employer is not vicariously liable for the discriminatory acts of an employee. But a failure to deal with an employee for making racist comments, even in their personal life, will mean the employer probably loses the ability to rely on that defence.

We have no specific policy for allowing employees to challenge their performance ratings but, as a matter of fairness, we allow these to be contested via a grievance. We have someone who's challenged their last rating, and the rating the year before. The former has been upheld and the rating will be overturned, but the latter hasn't been upheld due

to the passage of time, and the employee working for over a year without expressing dissatisfaction. They want to appeal. Do you think the employee has a fair challenge here?

I think there may be little merit in the appeal, but you should allow the employee to try. If you don't allow somebody an appeal from a grievance when you've allowed them to take out a grievance, that is a potential constructive dismissal. It's certainly in breach of the Acas Code of Practice (Acas Code), which is a prima facie constructive dismissal. The Acas Code says that you have to allow the employee an appeal.

Your refusal to overturn the year-old performance rating because it wasn't challenged for a year will normally be perfectly reasonable, and you can uphold that decision on appeal. However, if the employee has a good reason for not challenging it within the initial year (and not wanting to rock the boat is unlikely to suffice), then it's sensible to review the original assessment carefully and fairly if you want to retain someone who might be a good employee.

In a redundancy case, must an employee specifically raise bumping before an employer needs to consider it?

The *Maraab v Mentor Graphics (EAT/0172/17)* case says that if your decision not to consider bumping (or transferred redundancy) falls within the range of reasonable responses, then you don't need to actively consider it. Do you think it's reasonable not to consider a subordinate role with lesser terms? If your answer to that is yes, and you're confident you can justify that to a tribunal, then it doesn't need to be considered.

If you're not confident that you could justify that to a tribunal, then you should consider it. Of course, considering bumping doesn't mean you have to bump. You can think about it and then decide you're not going to do it. That's all that the duty to consider bumping involves. It's not very onerous. Just keep a note of your reasons in case you are ever challenged.

You can choose to offer to bump somebody (especially if they've got under two years' employment) and let the potentially redundant employee decide, but as long as you've got reasonable grounds for not bumping, then your decision not to offer it will fall within the range of reasonable responses.

A client is transferring eight employees to a new company. The new company has requested to start redundancy before the transfer. How would this work?

If anyone is made redundant because of the transfer, liability transfers automatically to the transferee, the receiving company. So if the employees are redundant before TUPE day, and I'm assuming TUPE applies, then the new company is liable anyway, even if the employees were made redundant by the old company. In terms of the process for redundancy, it's just a question of using common sense. There's got to be consultation, and the old company has to effectively facilitate the new company coming in and doing the consultation.

We have staff that submit timesheets for hours worked or for overtime claims, and then, separate to that, expenses. Is there a time frame that we can put on staff claiming these hours or expenses? There's nothing currently in the contracts.

If you have nothing in their contracts limiting the time they have to make claims, then it's unlimited, which means you would have to introduce a new term into their contracts. That might be a little tricky, but there are ways of doing it.

There's absolutely no reason why you shouldn't impose a timeframe. Many employers do. It's a pure matter of contract, so in theory, you could say that new employees have to make claims within the same month or the next month, otherwise their claims won't be paid. In reality, most employers would exercise discretion and say, 'submit it in by the month end, following the month in which it's incurred, but we have the discretion to pay it if you submit it within the three months after that.'

If you are changing terms and conditions of employment to introduce a new provision – a new timeframe – you're essentially reducing the employees' pay. That's really what you're doing. You're saying, "We would have paid you £100 before this, but now we're only going to pay you £75 because you didn't tick the boxes we wanted you to tick."

So, the tribunal will need to be persuaded that you have a good compelling business reason for the change, and it will also need to balance the interests of the employee and the interests of the employer when you're trying to impose a change of terms and conditions.

Now, you can probably show a good business reason, but in order to help you with the balancing act, it's better to have a slightly more generous timeframe, maybe three months. Of course, you only need to worry about the balancing act if employees won't agree to it. I'd have thought that with changed contracts like this, the majority of employees would be happy to sign on the dotted line because nobody actually thinks to themselves, "I'm going to put in my expense claim late." It's in nobody's interest to do that. The employees want their claims to be paid.

A contractor served us notice that they would no longer provide cleaning services. On the last day of their three months' notice period, they've told us about staff they believe TUPE to us (and apparently their staff now think they work for us). What is the legal position of them taking on an employee to work on our contract, after they've given us notice, please?

The employee has TUPE rights because if they are assigned to work on that contract, then their employment will automatically transfer. However, if their assigning to the contact isn't sufficiently permanent — so, for example, they've been assigned to other contracts and they've just been assigned to your contract the day before, perhaps as a 'poison pill' — then you would have a decent argument under TUPE that they haven't actually been assigned to the contract that's moved back to you. In order for someone's employment to move over, they have to be assigned to the contract that's being moved, or being taken back in-house in your case.

I have a self-employed person working for me, generating sales. They have lots of freedom; they

do their own thing really. They have the use of a company vehicle, which they use for travel for work and to and from home. Could this, on its own, determine whether they're an employee as opposed to self-employed?

It's a factor. Provision of a company car is something that points to the person being an employee. Providing a company car isn't in itself going to make the person an employee, if everything else points towards them being self-employed, but it's a factor that points towards employment status, and there's just no way around that.

Can you compel someone to be a witness in an employment tribunal?

Yes. Anybody can apply to a tribunal for a witness order compelling an individual based in England and Wales to attend. All the claimant needs to do is write to the tribunal. This is one of those rare occasions where the Respondent doesn't get copied in. The application should state that "X person is refusing to give evidence and their evidence is relevant for the following reasons (list reasons). Please issue a witness order." The tribunal will compel the witness to attend almost as a matter of course if they think the witness will be relevant.

Also by Daniel Barnett

Available on Amazon

JOIN DANIEL EVERY SATURDAY EVENING AT
9PM WHEN HE PRESENTS THE

LBC Legal Hour
— OR CATCH UP VIA THE GLOBAL PLAYER,
AT bit.ly/lbclegalhour

SATURDAYS, 9PM

I have updated my 20 Employment Law Policies for small businesses.

If you are an HR professional, they are perfect for incorporating into a staff handbook. If you are a solicitor, they come with a licence for you to resell them or give them away for free to clients.

HR INNER CIRCLE

"The HR Inner Circle has improved my life amazingly,

mainly because it means I have to spend less time researching and more time and more time actually doing the work I'm paid for."

Sue Whittle, Employment & Safety Advice LTD

Join to gain access to the monthly HR Inner Circular magazine

jam-packed with amazing information for ambitious HR professionals

WWW.HRINNERCIRCLE.CO.UK

What do you get?

1 Monthly live online 'Ask Me Anything' sessions: each month, we host an online video webinar, when you can share your HR problems and ask Daniel anything about employment law. You'll also receive a recording and a transcript each month, so you have a permanent record of the session even if you cannot be there.

———DANIEL BARNETT'S———
(HR) INNER CIRCLE

Please ask your questions now:
1. click 'Raise Hand'; or,
2. type it into the Questions box

"Daniel Barnett is an inspirational, walking and talking 'how to understand mind-boggling employment law handbook!"

Ellie King, HR Manager, RWE Technology

2 A specially recorded audio seminar every month, with HR shortcuts and workarounds you can't get anywhere else.

3 The monthly Inner Circular magazine, jam-packed with valuable information for ambitious HR professionals.

4 Access to Daniel's exclusive, private, invitation-only online Inner Circle group, where you get to discuss HR problems with other smart, ambitious professionals and download precedents and policies they have shared.

"It's the support and help that you get, the reassurance that you're talking to people who know what they're talking about rather than people just randomly giving information."

Nicky Jolley, HR2DAY LTD

5 Access to the exclusive HR Inner Circle website which includes a back-catalogue of all the HRIC resources since the launch in 2015.

WWW.HRINNERCIRCLE.CO.UK

"This is one of the best investments in yourself and your career you will ever decide to take."

100%
Risk-Free
Guarantee

Only **£86 + VAT** per month

No long-term contracts.
No notice periods.
No fuss.

Join today!

If you are looking for a forum to discuss confidential issues that need prompt employment law advice, then the HR Inner Circle is definitely for you. In addition it offers other tools to help and support. The Facebook group is full of information and solutions to scenarios — invaluable for HR professionals.

- **Sheena Doyle**, Managing Director, The Really Useful HR Company Ltd

It's a forum where you're not afraid to ask stupid questions, even though I'm not usually afraid of doing that. The sheer variety of experience and skillsets ensures there is always an informed discussion. JOIN NOW!!

- **Jon Dews**, HR & Business Partner, Majestic 12 Ltd

If you are looking for a steady stream of thorough, pragmatic, and easily-digestible employment law advice, the HR Inner Circle is a great place to be.

- **Susi O'Brien**, Senior Manager HR, The Action Group

The regular updates are invaluable to not only me, but also my team. We find that they are presented in an easy to digest format and aren't too 'legalistic'.

- **Donna Negus**, Sekoya Specialist Employment Services

There aren't many other employment law advice services where you get direct access to an employment law barrister at a realistic price. Join the HR Inner Circle now – you won't regret it.

- **Kirsten Cluer**, Owner of Cluer HR, HR Consultancy

I like being able to use the HR Inner Circle Facebook group to ask other members for a second opinion, or for ideas when I get stuck with solving a tricky situation. There's usually someone who has come across the situation before.

- **Helen Astill**, Managing Director, Cherington HR Ltd

When I transitioned from big employers to an SME, I didn't realise how much I would miss having peers to kick ideas around. If you haven't got an internal network, you've got to build an external one. I got so much out of the discussion at an Inner Circle meetup recently and I look forward to getting the Inner Circular.

- **Elizabeth Divver**, Group HR Director, The Big Issue Group

Sign now! The monthly Q & A sessions are invaluable, the magazine is packed full of helpful info, you get lots of goodies and the Facebook page is really informative and a useful sounding board.

- **Caroline Hitchen**, Consultant, Caroline Neal Employment Law

Being a member of HR Inner Circle is one of the best sources of HR information and advice, and receiving the monthly audio seminars and magazines is extremely helpful and interesting. I can't recommend becoming a member highly enough. There is a private Facebook group which is great for asking other members advice and sharing knowledge and experiences. I have also recently attended one of the meetups that is organised by Daniel Barnett, and it was good to meet other members (and of course Daniel) in a more social setting. It was also a good opportunity to ask any questions you wanted and being able to get advice or support as to how they would deal with whatever you ask.

- **Tracey Seymour**, HR Manager (Head of Dept), Kumon Europe & Africa Ltd

The help and advice from other HR professionals on Facebook is really valuable, and quick. All the team enjoy the audio seminars and magazines for updates on current issues.

- **Catherine Larke**, Director | myHRdept.co.uk

For me it's a no brainer. We have a lot of really good contributors in the HR Inner Circle and it's more than a discussion forum and invaluable source of information. When combined with the magazine, the audio seminars and events, it is a complete service especially with Daniel's legal expertise always on hand.

- **Elizabeth Ince**, Self employed HR Consultant

Just join! It is invaluable with the resources you have at hand by joining the HR Inner Circle. Especially the Facebook Group where you can get advice or a different point of view that you may not have previously considered, outside of normal working hours which is very useful. Live Q&A's too.

- **Diana Wilks**, HR Manager, Go South Coast Ltd

HR can be complex because each and every issue will have its own set of individual circumstances. Being in the HR Inner Circle enables you to bounce ideas around and make sure you are considering every angle and aspect, knowing your HR Inner Circle partners will have had a similar experience to share.

- **Pam Rogerson**, HR Director, ELAS Group

Printed in Great Britain
by Amazon